The LIFE CYCLES Library

The LIFE CYCLE of a MOUSE

Andrew Hipp

The Rosen Publishing Group's
PowerKids Press™
New York

For my dearest Rachel - Andrew Hipp
To my granddaughter Meghan - Dwight Kuhn

Published in 2002 by The Rosen Publishing Group, Inc.
29 East 21st Street, New York, NY 10010

First Edition

Book Design: Michael Caroleo and Michael de Guzman
Project Editor: Emily Raabe

Photo credits: All photos © Dwight Kuhn

Hipp, Andrew.
   The life cycle of a mouse / Andrew Hipp.
    p. cm.— (The life cycles library)
   Includes index.
   Summary: This book describes the physical characteristics, behavior, and reproduction of white-footed mice.
   ISBN 0-8239-5866-3
   1. Mice—Life cycles—Juvenile literature. [1. Mice.] I. Title. II. Series.
    QL737.R6 H63 2002   2001-1119
    599.35—dc21

Manufactured in the United States of America

Contents

Making a Home

Male and female white-footed mice work together to build a nest for their family. The nest is usually round and is made of grass and leaves. It may be hidden beneath a log, among vines, or in an old, underground, woodchuck burrow. The inside of the nest often is lined with soft fur, feathers, cloth, or plant parts. The nest is about the size of a big grapefruit. When their nest gets dirty, mice leave it and build a new one. White-footed mice usually build several nests in a year.

◄ *Mouse nests have one small doorway at the top of the nest. In winter, mice build bigger nests to protect them from the cold.*

Just Born

Female white-footed mice have from one to four **litters** every year. There are usually three or four mice in each litter, but there can be from one to seven babies. The mother mouse is pregnant for about 23 days. After her litter is born, she can become pregnant again in one or two days. Newborn mice can't move around by themselves. They can't see or hear, and they are almost bald. Their only food is their mother's milk. They drink her milk by nursing.

These helpless pups will squeak and chirp to get their mother's attention. ▶

Four Days Old

The pups begin to grow fur when they are four days old. They can crawl a little bit and bury themselves beneath their warm siblings. They can't see or hear clearly. If someone tickles one of their whiskers, the babies can feel it. At this age, however, they still don't know where the tickle comes from. The pups' first teeth appear from four to seven days after birth. Their teeth are strong and they help the pups hold onto their mother when she nurses them.

◀ *These baby mice cannot see or hear, because their eyes and ears are still closed.*

Family Life

A mother mouse nurses her pups until they are three or four weeks old. The pups grow very quickly during this time. The mother carries her pups in her mouth to move them. She needs to protect her pups because other mice may try to hurt or kill unprotected babies. Fathers do not help raise the pups. They usually leave the nest when the litter is born. After one month of nursing, the pups begin to eat solid food.

When she needs to leave the nest, the mother mouse stretches herself gently to release her pups. ▶

Leaving the Nest

At five weeks old, a pup is old enough to live on its own. At this point, either the pups leave the nest or the mother leaves to build another nest for her next litter. When pups leave the nest, they look for mates to start their own families. Male pups travel farther from the nest than their sisters do in search of a mate. If pups are born in the winter, they may stay in the nest for up to two months to keep warm with the rest of their family.

◄ *White-footed mice are usually ready to start a family when they are about seven weeks old.*

Growing Teeth

A mouse's front teeth, or **incisors**, never stop growing. They grow throughout a mouse's life. These teeth allow mice to eat hard foods such as acorns, nuts, insects, and seeds. These hard foods wear down the incisors. If a mouse's incisors stopped growing, the teeth would wear away completely. Only rabbits and **rodents** such as white-footed mice, squirrels, hamsters, gerbils, guinea pigs, and beavers have incisors that continue to grow.

If mice and other rodents don't gnaw hard food, their teeth may grow so long that they can no longer eat. ▶

Nightlife in the Forest

White-footed mice are **nocturnal** and rarely are seen during the day. They depend on their hearing and sharp eyesight to avoid danger. When they sense trouble, white-footed mice may beat the ground with their front paws to warn other mice. They can run very fast from **predators**, often leaping like small squirrels or rabbits. Even though they run fast, they do not always escape danger. Owls, hawks, snakes, coyotes, and other animals all eat white-footed mice.

◀ *White-footed mice almost never walk anywhere. Instead they leap and run from place to place.*

Mice and People

Mice can carry diseases, such as **Lyme disease**, that harm people. Lyme disease is caused by **bacteria** that are passed from a mouse to a tick. The tick then bites a person and passes the disease to the person. When mouse populations get too large, the diseases they carry spread rapidly. Hawks, owls, snakes, coyotes, and foxes all help keep mouse populations small because they eat mice. By eating mice, these predators slow the spread of diseases.

Mice sometimes eat people's food. They also can be very helpful, however, eating insects that otherwise would feed on crops. ▶

Winter

White-footed mice do not **hibernate**. They spend the winter looking for food and eating from **caches**, hiding places where they store food. Some mice eat all the food in their caches in one or two months. Other caches last longer. A lucky squirrel might find and eat a cache. If this happens, the mouse must look for more food. Mice spend much of the winter in tunnels that they dig beneath the snow. The snow acts like a blanket and keeps them warm.

◀ *White-footed mice and some other mammals store heat in the form of special fat, which they burn in the winter to keep warm. They also keep warm by shivering, just like people do.*

21

White-Footed Mice and Their Relatives

The **ancestors** of white-footed mice appeared in North America about 33 million years ago. Today more than 350 different **species** of mice live in North and South America. You can look for white-footed mice and their relatives in fields, shrubby thickets, and wood lots. You may find their old nests filled with tiny scat, or poop, the size of rice grains. You may find footprints in the snow or pinecones chewed to pieces by hungry mice. If you are patient and spend a lot of time outdoors, you may even see a white-footed mouse up close.

Glossary

ancestors (AN-ses-turz) Relatives who lived long ago.

bacteria (bak-TEER-ee-uh) Tiny living things that can be seen only with a microscope.

caches (KASH-iz) Hiding places, usually for food.

hibernate (HY-bur-nayt) To spend the winter sleeping or resting.

incisors (in-SY-zerz) The front teeth of mammals, made especially for cutting food.

litters (LIH-turz) A group of babies born to the same mother at the same time.

Lyme disease (LYM dih-ZEEZ) A sickness carried by many mammals, especially deer and white-footed mice. People catch it only from ticks that have bitten an infected animal.

nocturnal (nok-TER-nul) Active during the night.

predators (PREH-duh-terz) Animals that kill other animals for food.

rodents (RO-dints) An order of mammals who all have sharp incisors that never stop growing as long as they are alive. Most rodents are small and eat plant life.

species (SPEE-sheez) A single kind of plant, animal, or other living thing.

Index

Web Sites

To learn more about mice, check out these Web sites:

www.nsrl.ttu.edu/tmot1/peroleuc.htm

www.rmca.org/